C000142353

THE
FISHING
BOATS
STORY

Colourful fishing vessels at Maryport in north-west England. These add colour to any harbour around the country.

THE
FISHING
BOATS
STORY

MIKE SMYLIE

The
History
Press

For Christoffer, Ana & Otis

First published 2017

The History Press
The Mill, Brimscombe Port
Stroud, Gloucestershire, GL5 2QG
www.thehistorypress.co.uk

© Mike Smylie, 2017

The right of Mike Smylie to be identified as the Author
of this work has been asserted in accordance with the
Copyright, Designs and Patents Act 1988.

All rights reserved. No part of this book may be reprinted
or reproduced or utilised in any form or by any electronic,
mechanical or other means, now known or hereafter invented,
including photocopying and recording, or in any information
storage or retrieval system, without the permission in writing
from the Publishers.

British Library Cataloguing in Publication Data.
A catalogue record for this book is available from the British Library.

ISBN 978 0 7509 6997 0

Typesetting and origination by The History Press
Printed in Turkey

All photographs from the author's collection
unless otherwise credited.

Cover illustrations. Front: By the 1950s
and '60s the hull shape of the ringers had
broadened and lengthened, largely because
of the increase in engine power. The method
of fishing remained constant, although
innovations improved catches. Here the
Village Maid II, TT25, built by Nobles of
Girvan in 1961, measured almost 59ft. *Back:*
These 'scaffies' off Wick show influence from
across the North Sea.

CONTENTS

It's fair to say that most people will visit, or have visited, a fishing harbour at some time in their life and will be, or have been, attracted to the colourful array of fishing vessels. As a maritime nation, we are naturally drawn to the coast even if many of us don't like actually being on the sea. Harbours are halfway houses, a place betwixt land and sea, and are always a scene of action, whether it's a boat landing fish or one being discussed over by a group of old seadogs! In the days of sail, the harbours were stuffed with boats and an oft-heard saying is that it was possible to walk across the harbour over the fishing boats. This was likely true for most British harbours at some time in the fishing calendar.

We are very lucky in Britain: we have seen a huge selection of diverse fishing craft working the coastal waters over several centuries. Much of the diversity lies in the topographical make-up of the coast which in itself is magnificently vibrant – more so in reality. Study any map and it's pretty clear that we have a great mixture over what is a vast coastline. There are soft golden sand beaches where the tide goes out for miles; there are rock-strewn coasts with little shelter which the west winds bombard almost ceaselessly; then small river estuaries where good harbour facilities have been built; larger estuaries with treacherous sandbanks lying offshore waiting for unwitting vessels; cute pebbly beaches where boats are drawn up away from the surf; shelf platforms preventing access; islands with man-made harbours; bays where man has built quays for protection; exposed inland seas such as Morecambe Bay; and tiny fishing communities sitting almost in the sea ... However you look at it, there is a huge variety throughout the whole of the 20,000-odd miles of British coastline.

Working boats, and especially fishing craft, have evolved through time according to the very nature of the coast they work from. The Vikings brought their traditions, as did fishermen from other countries who fished within sight of these shores. But fish have no respect for boundaries and, in a similar way, neither did fishermen until countries instigated their own territorial waters. The design of these boats depended on factors such as whether there was a harbour to land, or a beach to be drawn up; the type of sea to be encountered – western Atlantic or eastern North Sea as there's a great difference – the method or methods of fishing to be worked; and the available funds to finance the boat. Then there was tradition in the way a particular custom of boat had been handed down through the generations from father to son. Often this had been influenced by cultures such as the Viking age or Dutch command. On the other hand, some fishermen

had developed their own ideas of innovation which had influenced the design whilst, at the same time, some boatbuilders had, too, their own ideas which they translated into the particular boat they were building. A mass of differentials, then, that all add up to a rich mixture of vessels of all sizes working the various fisheries.

DID YOU KNOW?

Herring comes from the word '*heer*', meaning 'army' in Old German, because of the size of shoals they swam in.

Since time immemorial wood has been instrumental in boatbuilding, although early hide or skin boats perhaps contradict the assertion that wooden boats were solely built of wood. Exclude the hide boats for now, and the flat-bottomed boats mentioned by writers in the Roman period and before were generally exclusively wooden. Wood certainly prevailed until the advent of the iron steam trawlers of the late nineteenth century. Wood maintained its dominance until both fibreglass and steel craft became popular in the second half of the twentieth century. But by this time regional variations had become insignificant and trends were being nationally adopted throughout the industry.

◀◀ Port Seton harbour, near Edinburgh, full of fishing vessels. In the background is a boatbuilding yard. Many of these boats would have been built locally.

Of course, the advent of the internal combustion engine had a major impact on fishing boat design, as it did across all the various sectors of British (and world) life. Previously, sail and oared vessels were the only option, depending on the area of operation. River craft had little use of any other motive power and some remain so today. But, as sail was deposed by motor and the older boats disappeared, the spirit of some of the wonderfully romantic-looking craft have survived into the twenty-first century for us to admire today in all their splendour.

Little documented evidence exists for the earliest fishing craft, but it is generally accepted that skin craft were used in rivers and close to the shore. Wooden boats, such as those unearthed in various archaeological sites around Britain, prove that planked boats have been in existence for thousands of years.

➤➤ Upturned boats on Holy Island, Northumberland. Many an old boat was turned turtle and placed ashore to provide a shed for a fisherman's gear, thus enabling a vessel to continue its usefulness well beyond its seaworthiness. (Courtesy of Carle Robinson)

DID YOU KNOW?

In 2016 there were some 2,000 small (under 10m) vessels fishing only 4 per cent of the UK quota. How unfair is that! They represent some 75 per cent of the total fleet.

When the Norsemen arrived on these shores in the eighth century, they came with their clinker-built craft and yet there is some evidence to say that such vessels were already in use in Britain, brought to us by the Saxons of northern parts of today's Germany. Boats were either propelled with oars and/or sails, and, as such, details of these don't really surface until the seventeenth century. We will therefore begin with the development of sailing fishing craft from that time into the eighteenth and nineteenth centuries.

The boats in this book are mainly of the wooden variety, although steel and fibreglass fishing boats superseded the previous huge array of wooden boats. While these ubiquitous boats are mentioned – no story would be complete without them – they do represent the 'end of the line' of a tradition, as boats from any one place are similar to others from another. They are workhorses of great magnitude, bristling with both navigational gear and mechanical equipment. Like every other corner of industry, they are purposeful and technological. They employ fewer people than the older boats, but that's by no way unique, as it is the way of today's world. We can watch it but it doesn't mean we have to like it!

A word of warning: with fishing boats being such a diverse group of vessels, it is impossible to show all of them in such a small book. Thus there will be many variations of type that are missing. This is by no means an omission, simply an illustration of how far and wide their use has been over time. *The Fishing Boats Story* attempts to highlight the main types from which the others have evolved. Whereas modern fishing boats tend to obey similar sets of rules, for sailing fishing boats there were no rules – simply a desire to catch fish, carry it home and, hopefully, arrive safely. Many didn't, and still today fishing remains the country's most dangerous occupation. Thus, to all those lost fishermen, this book is dedicated.

SCOTLAND

In the eighteenth and nineteenth centuries, Scotland had an almost unlimited supply of fish in the waters that surrounded its coast. However, given the huge variation in the make-up of its coast, there were many different types of sailing craft dedicated solely to one of the different methods of fishing, though, of course, there were times when these same boats were used for transport amongst the islands and inaccessible parts of the coast that had no land-based infrastructure. From the North Sea-facing east coast to the indented western side, and from rugged northern Shetland to the less harsh Orkney Isles, the diversity is rich.

The 'Great Boat' was said to be the earliest inshore boat of the eighteenth century, a two-masted boat of about 40ft in length. To fish the herring fishery offshore, the herring buss worked a fishery model copied from the Dutch. These busses, some 50–70 tons in weight, were capable of staying at sea for several weeks, even months,

DID YOU KNOW?

The mainmast of a Scottish fifie or Zulu was so big that a man could hardly reach around it at deck level.

crewed by around twelve men. When the government introduced bounties to encourage the herring fishery in 1750, these busses had to assemble at either Bressay Sound, off Shetland, in June or Campbeltown, in the west, in September, and remain fishing to receive a set amount per barrel of herring landed.

When the bounty system was changed in 1786 to encourage herring fishing in small boats, there was equal encouragement to build herring towns around the coast – namely at Tobermory, Uig, Ullapool and, later, at Wick. Only the latter two met with any success, and yet the herring fishery became, for Scottish fishermen, a bonanza.

The Northern Isles

However, sometimes it is forgotten that it wasn't just herring that enabled coastal dwellers to survive through the fruits of the sea. A good example of this was in Shetland where fishermen – although they were under the control of the landowner fraternity – sailed out some 30 miles offshore in their open boats to set long lines for bottom-feeding fish such as cod and ling. The boats the Shetlanders used were influenced by the Norsemen for, in treeless Shetland which was geographically nearer to the harbours of Norway than to the main centres of population such as Aberdeen, the boats came directly from Scandinavia. In time the

➤ A small foureen-type Shetland boat built by Tommy Isbister in the 1990s, showing that these designs are based on age-old traditions.

Shetlanders learnt to build their own, first in kit form that they imported and eventually just using Norwegian timber. The boats exhibit the same influences today. For the deep-sea fishery – the *haaf* as they called it – they used the six-oared sixareen, whilst the inshore boat was the four-oared fourereen. Both of these types were rigged with square-topped lugsail. Off the south coast, around Sumburgh Head, with its strong tides, the fishermen developed their *Ness* yoles. Meanwhile, on the small island of Fair Isle halfway between Shetland and Orkney, they developed their own Fair Isle skiff for fishing, rigged with a square sail. In Orkney two types of boat evolved, both being known as yoles. In the north they were rigged with two lugsails whilst in the south they were slightly larger, fuller in the stern and rigged with two spritsails. Orkney boats seem to have been a merging of Shetland and mainland Scottish traditions in hull shape.

▼ Clinker-built Orkney yoles have enjoyed a renaissance in recent years and here two 'new' boats are sailing on regatta day at Stromness in about 2002.

▼ Here on St Mary's, on the southernmost part of Mainland, are two Orkney yoles and a fifie, locally called a 'firthie'.

West Coast

On the west coast, Loch Fyne has been the centre of a rich fishery for centuries. Various open skiffs were used for line-fishing and drift-netting for herring. When a particular method of fishing called the ring-net – a form of trawling – was introduced in the 1830s, the design of fishing boats altered slightly to suit the method. This trawl skiff then evolved through an increase in size into the half-decked Lochfyne skiff. Meanwhile, double-ended boats, often called *bata* in Gaelic (i.e. 'boat') were commonplace throughout the rest of the west coast.

In the Outer Hebrides, at the northern end of the Isle of

◄ The Lochfyne skiff *Fairy Brae*, 55CN, off Davaar Island, Campbeltown, *c*.1890. These skiffs were larger versions of the typical west coast double-enders which, being half-decked, allowed crews some accommodation under the forecastle.

◄ Landing the catch at Ullapool. The nearest boat is a typical west coast type generally called a *bata*, which translates to 'boat'. Behind is a *sgoth* registered at Stornoway.

Lewis, where, like the Shetlanders, fishermen sailed offshore to fish long-lines, a *sgoth Niseach* – literally 'Ness skiff' – became the favoured boat working from the small tidal harbour of Ness. It was renowned as the largest beach boat in Britain. Further south, the tiny island of Grimsay built its own Grimsay lobster boat for fishing with creels off the Monach Islands. Similar line boats worked from various other Outer Hebrides creeks and harbours.

East Coast

On the east coast, the two early nineteenth-century boats were the scaffie in the north and the fifie from the south. Both were double-ended lug-rigged boats, the first having similarities to the northern isles boats, developed again from Norse influence. The more upright fifies are said to have been influenced by Dutch vessels. Both of these types

> **DID YOU KNOW?**
>
> In 1872, in England, Scotland, Wales, Ireland and the Isle of Man there were nearly 42,000 registered fishing boats. In 2014 this figure was 6,383 boats for the UK.

◄◄ The *sgoth Niseach An Sulaire* sailing hard along the Harris coast. These skiffs were the largest British boats to work off beaches, primarily because the harbour at Ness was so silted up the tide often never allowed enough water in the harbour to sail directly out. This replica vessel was built in 1994. (Courtesy of *An Sulaire* Trust)

➤ This Wick-registered fifie was typical of the larger boats that worked trains of herring nets. The development of the Ironman capstan, seen by the mizzen mast, allowed longer nets to be set instead of only using manpower to haul in.

grew in length as building methods, such as carvel construction, improved in the nineteenth century and decked craft became the norm. Fifies were in excess of 70ft, whilst in Shetland these fifies tended to be gaff rigged.

◄ The fifie *Swan*, LK243, restored in more recent times, was typical of many of the Shetland fifies in that they adopted the gaff rig over the lug rig because of the tidal waters around the islands.

◄◄ A mixture of fifies and Zulus in Portgordon harbour. Each is discerned by the shape of the sternpost: fifies are upright and Zulus sloping.

In the 1870s both types were merged into one in the superbly designed Zulu craft, a vessel ultimately in excess of 80ft, rigged with two huge dipping lugsails on massive unsupported masts. Although these are regarded as being the pinnacle of sailing fishing boat design, they were short-lived as the dawn of the new era of motorised vessels was about to change the face of fishing forever.

EAST COAST OF ENGLAND

As far as the offshore fleet was concerned, early boats fishing the North Sea were lug-rigged Yorkshire yawls and Norfolk luggers, superseding the earlier three-masted luggers. These boats primarily drifted for herring, dropping the mainmast when they lay to their nets, although they also long-lined out of the herring season. In the second part of the nineteenth century these generally adopted the dandy rig of a lug main and gaff mizzen. Ten years later, with the massive expansion in trawling in the North Sea for white fish, they all switched to a gaff-rigged ketch layout, which proved more powerful for towing the trawls. Similar vessels worked out of Hull and Grimsby as the North Sea fishery spread along the coast. Amazingly, in 1858, there were more than 840 boats working

◄ The ketch-rigged Lowestoft trawler *Excelsior*, LT472, is typical of the sailing trawlers working the waters of the North Sea and many others originated from Grimsby, Hull and Ramsgate. (Courtesy of Excelsior Trust)

out of Grimsby, which had become the biggest fish port in the world by the end of that century.

The inshore sector saw a variation in types along this coast. In Northumberland and Yorkshire it was the coble that fished: drifting for herring, setting lobster and crab pots, long-lining as well as trawling. The lug-rigged coble was unique amongst British craft in that it had a ramplank instead of the after part of the keel. In essence it was a cross between a flat-bottomed boat and a keelboat. It evolved from the need to work directly off the beaches and launch into the surf – a process that it perfected. A larger version was a plosher, which was regarded as a herring boat and is said to have

▶▶ The Yorkshire coble here is *Gratitude* at Robin Hood's Bay and is perfectly presented by the photographer in a well-planned photo. The shape is easy to understand, having a flat bottom to remain upright on the beach, a deep bow to cut into the waves and a flat transom to act kindly in following seas.

DID YOU KNOW?

The letters and numbers painted on fishing boats are their registration letters and numbers. The letters refer to the port of registry (usually the first and last letter, e.g. Peterhead is PD) and the number is allocated by the registrar and is unique to that vessel from that particular port.

▲ The similarity in hull shape of these Cromer crabbers to the coble is obvious, although they have a continuous keel and retain the pointed stern. They have been compared with beach boats across the North Sea on the west coast of Denmark.

got its name from the practice of beating the bows with a rope to drive the fish into the net. These were half decked and set a single lugsail. A mule was a hybrid – a mixture of a keelboat and a coble – the influence coming from the older whaling boats seen sailing from harbours such as Whitby.

Norfolk was home to a healthy crab fishery, centred on Cromer and Sheringham, and a double-ended vessel developed primarily for this: the Cromer crab boat. Neither place had a harbour and the fishermen worked straight off the beach. These boats were recognisable by the method they were carried into, and out of, the sea by the fishermen: with the oars placed horizontally through holes in the gunwale, called the orrucks. Although built on a keel, these boats do show a resemblance to the cobles from up the coast. Norfolk punts worked cockle, mussel and oyster beds around places such as Brancaster Staithe.

Lynn yolls also collected cockles and mussels around the Wash.

◄ Two Yarmouth shrimpers at Ipswich in about 1998, the shrimp trawl lying on the deck of the nearest boat. These gaff-rigged beamy boats had a small cuddy for basic shelter."

Based in King's Lynn, they shared the harbour with Wash smacks, which generally dredged oysters. Others were based in Boston from out of where shrimpers worked. Paull, on the river Humber, also had a small fleet of shrimpers.

A fleet of beamy Yarmouth shrimpers worked the shallow water around that port. Yarmouth and Lowestoft both became major herring ports with hundreds of boats landing there during the autumnal herring season, when boats from Scotland and as far as Cornwall came to join the bonanza. Local boats were generally lug-rigged for drifting whilst large ketch-rigged trawlers, similar to those from Grimsby, were also based at the two ports. Along the Suffolk coast, punts fished off the beaches for species such as herring and sprats, working as far down as the river Deben, where it could be said we enter the confines of the Thames estuary.

THAMES ESTUARY

For the sake of clarity, it can be said that the Thames estuary stretches from the river Deben over to the North Foreland on the north-west tip of Kent. It is generally accepted that the Peter boats were the original fishing boats of the river Thames itself and documented evidence of their use first surfaces in the sixteenth century. By the nineteenth century, rigged with one

◄◄ The Suffolk beach boat LT790 is perhaps similar in shape to the shrimpers to the untrained eye, though are not as beamy and deep in shape. They worked the coast from just south of Lowestoft to the river Deben in various fisheries – sprats, herring, trawling, shrimping and potting.

> The Leigh cockle boat *Mary Amelia*, LO502, after restoration. Similar to the Thames bawleys, these open boats were beached on the cockle banks, loaded by hand, and sailed back to Leigh to unload, and are thus relatively flat-bottomed. (Courtesy of Robert Simper)

spritsail, they were fishing out into the estuary and were some 30ft in length with a small cuddy beneath a short foredeck. They also had a wet well – one of the first boats to have holes drilled in the planking to allow seawater to flood a compartment, into which fish could be placed to remain fresh.

The Thames bawley is regarded as a later development: a shallow, long-keeled vessel used to catch shrimp over the shoal water. Their name is accepted to be a corruption of 'boiler', an installation used to cook the shrimps direct from the sea.

Leigh-on-Sea today remains renowned for its cockles. Initially any old boat was used to sail out to the sandbanks and manually collect cockles. Purpose-built craft appeared around the turn of the twentieth century, when a Leigh cockle boat resembled a bawley, similarly rigged though largely open to allow the shellfish to be loaded aboard.

One of the best-known sailing fishing boats is the Essex smack. These came in varying sizes and followed as varied fishing. The smallest class, at under 35ft, generally worked oyster dredges and trawled, whilst the next size up – to about 50ft – fished in the rivers for sprats with a stow-net (a complicated net affair spread out beneath the boat) and dredged for oysters, trawled offshore. The biggest examples fished away, sailing as far as Luce Bay, the Menai Strait, Swansea, the river Fal, off Fife,

◄ The 1904-built *Emeline*, F14, is a typical oyster dredger from Whitstable, although these are harder in the bilge than those from the Essex coast where there were many more. The Kent boats were more used to sitting upright in Kentish muddy inlets.

DID YOU KNOW?

Before technology, herring were spotted by what the fishermen called the natural appearances. They looked for oil on the water or phosphorescence created by the herring shoals. Predators such as basking sharks also directed them to the shoals. At night the sound of gannets diving for the fish alerted them, and the sound of that dive could even identify the depth of the shoal.

the Norfolk coast and away over to Holland, especially off Terschelling where they gained the nickname skillingers. Smacks are regarded as fast, seaworthy vessels – probably one reason that many have survived.

Oyster dredgers also worked out of Whitstable and Faversham, on the Kent coast, the latter being said to be home to the oldest oyster fishery in the world. Whitstable oyster yawls, as they were sometimes called, again worked dredges, varying in size as the Essex boats, sailing far and wide in their search for rich grounds.

Various inshore boats worked the estuary. The Medway doble is regarded as being a later version of the Peter boat, the name coming from 'double boat' in respect of the wet well dividing the boat in two. Small whelk boats worked from Whitstable whilst, over in Essex, small winkle boats were called winkle-brigs.

SOUTH COAST OF ENGLAND

Between the Thames and Cornwall, a host of different boats fished the rich Channel waters, as well as bigger craft sailing into the North Sea where trawling opened up a massive fishery. Although the earliest fishing boats were the large three-masted luggers that were similar to those from the east coast, and that sailed as far as Cornwall, the best-known fishing boats are perhaps the Brixham trawlers: large ketch-rigged vessels built in Devon, registered at either Brixham, Dartmouth or Plymouth, that sailed all around the coast to trawl as that method of fishing developed in the nineteenth century. These were similar to the Lowestoft trawlers, and many were also built at Ramsgate and Rye, the former being said to have had the best fishing fleet in the country in Elizabethan times even though it never developed as a fishing port of any substance. Several of these large trawlers have survived, including a handful based in Brixham today.

In Kent there were also limited fleets in harbours such as Margate, Broadstairs, St Margaret's Bay

➤ Two trawlers: on the left is *Keewaydin*, LT1192, built in Rye in 1913, and on the right is *Vigilance*, BM76, built by Uphams of Brixham in 1926 as one of the last of the types. Both worked the North Sea trawling grounds. (Courtesy of Bill Wakeham)

➤➤ Hastings has long been home to a vibrant beach-based fishery and here a typical Hastings lugger of the end of the nineteenth century is seen on the beach. The lute stern became popular as it helped lift the stern, though after 1892 the elliptical stern gained favour from yachting influence.

and Dover, whilst the fishermen of Folkestone seemed to have preferred the boats of Cornwall – many were ordered from Cornish builders whilst some were bought second-hand. Sussex beach boats were more squat and beamy, and Hastings still has perhaps the best known beach-based fleet of fishing boats in the country. In the nineteenth century there were several sizes of boats working the coast between here and Brighton and Shoreham. The bluff-shaped hog-boats were fully decked and up to 35ft in length, with living accommodation below. They were sprit-rigged, usually with two masts, and drift-netted for mackerel and herring, and trawled inshore. However, as the lug rig gained favour, the hoggies, as they were sometimes called, were found to be unsuitable, and a variant of the shape had the added advantage of bilge keels that both gave it better sea performance and allowed it

> The Itchen Ferry *Wonder*, SU120, sailing in 2010. *Wonder* was, in fact, a fine example of these craft and was built by the great Dan Hatcher in 1860, and has been lovingly restored with sails from Faversham. Daniel G. Hatcher, known as King Dan to his contemporaries, was a very successful builder of yachts at his Belvedere yard between 1845 and 1880, and thus his working boats were equally renowned for their speed.

to sit more upright on the beach. Smaller 28ft-long boats, called 28-boats or bogs, developed at Hastings, specially for trawling. Even smaller boats were the 15ft punts, similar to the Kent craft. Luggers also worked out of Worthing, Eastbourne and Newhaven. Bognor and Littlehampton had their own lobster boats that worked off Selsey Bill.

In and around the Solent, the Itchen Ferry was a cutter-rigged boat built in and around Southampton. Up to 30ft in length, with a small cuddy beneath the short foredeck, these boats fished as far out as the south side of the Isle of Wight. Similar boats worked out of Portsmouth, Chichester and

◄◄ The Chesil Beach lerret *Sunday-at-Home* was typical of the seine-net boats that worked off the beach. Mackerel was the principal fishery. The boats were often rowed across the fleet, the water between the beach and the hinterland, and then launched into the surf. They retained the double end for this purpose.

Poole. Chichester was also, briefly, home to a particularly peculiar boat, the Chichester smack, only a few of which were built by local boatbuilder, timber merchant and fisherman J.D. Foster. Between 1880 and 1902 he built ten of these, the first being 55ft in length whilst his last, *Echo*, P76, was 110ft, and spent her years oyster dredging, until 1939. She ended up, like so many other fishing craft, being burnt on the beach on Guy Fawkes night.

West of Portland Bill, the Chesil Beach lerrets were small open boats that worked seine-nets for mackerel off the beach. They were largely owned by the seine companies, which consisted of up to fourteen members. A few lerrets are said to have sailed over to France, though the majority were simply rowed.

Devon has a rich maritime tradition that dates back to the days when boats sailed to Newfoundland, and more recently this tradition spread to the variety of fishing boats. We've already mentioned the large trawlers for which Brixham has become synonymous, but beach boats worked all along the coast. Smaller ketch-rigged trawlers were Brixham mules, whilst Mumble Bees were cutter-rigged vessels under 50ft. These seem to have originated from the Mumbles when the oyster fishery collapsed. Twelve smacks transferred to Brixham and these boats impressed the locals who then built their own versions.

➤➤ Today a small fleet still survives and races off the beach at Beer each summer, this one being the *Noddy*.

Beer had its own fleet of Beer luggers working off the beach, the earliest of which were three-masted. It is said that the Beer men created Brixham, who in turn opened up the North Sea fishery. Similar beach luggers worked from Sidmouth and Exmouth. In the South Hams, crabs were caught in quantity and small

▲ Small Devon beach boats worked from such beaches as Beer, the small village said to have pioneered trawling and having 'made Brixham', as the saying goes.

fleets of spritsailed open crabbers worked from Hallsands and Hope Cove. Plymouth had its own boats working out of Sutton Pool. The Plymouth hookers were heavily built gaffers, similar to many Cornish boats, where indeed many were built, which seems a convenient point to cross the river Tamar into that county.

CORNWALL

Cornwall's maritime past is all too often, all too unfairly and erroneously, associated with smuggling and wrecking along the rugged, wild coast. Contrary to this, it has a rich fishing history throughout its coast, north and south, as well as a tradition of sending seamen all over the world. Lacking roads throughout much of its exterior, it was the sea that people relied upon to get about. It was also home to the second biggest fishing fleet in the British Isles at one time, and today retains a strong presence in the fishing industry.

Evidence for its earliest boats comes from several depictions of square-rigged boats and, later, the three-masted luggers seen elsewhere in the Channel. By the second half of the nineteenth century, it was the Cornish lugger that fished, although operational influences created two distinct designs. In the eastern harbours of Looe, Polperro, Fowey and Mevagissey, the East

>> Double-ended St Ives pilchard boats were flatter in the hull shape than those from the south coast because of the drying nature of the harbour, as opposed to those that remained in water at all stages of the tide.

St Ives, Pilchard Boats.

Cornish luggers were transom-sterned. Further east, Polperro gaffers were, as the name implies, gaff-rigged boats on a very similar hull shape and were almost the same as the aforementioned Plymouth hookers. Originally sprit-rigged, they can be said to represent a meeting of traditions: the sprit rig from Devon and the lugger hull from the west.

To the west of the Lizard, the boats retained a bit of the Viking heritage and remained double-ended. Two types evolved, those working from the all-states-of-the-tide accessible harbours of Mount's Bay and those from tidal St Ives. The latter were full-bodied to sit upright once the tide had ebbed. Furthermore, the

DID YOU KNOW?
The replica Cornish lugger *Spirit of Mystery* was sailed to Australia by Pete Goss. This voyage, begun in 2008, mirrored that of the 37ft Newlyn lugger *Mystery* that completed the passage in 1854. Other Cornish luggers have sailed far and wide.

west Cornish often referred to their boats as drivers, as they regarded drifting with the tide as 'driving' the boat along.

Cornwall was once internationally famous for its pilchard fishery and hardly a coastal village was without its own pilchard cellars to cure the fish. Although the luggers drift-netted for pilchards, mackerel and herring, much of the pilchard catch was landed by seining, a method that dates back at least to the Middle Ages, and probably a lot earlier. Beach seining is one of man's first ways of catching fish, and seining at sea was simply an extension of that. Indeed, ring-netting, which is used to catch pilchards today, is itself a form of seining, even though

◀ Here that shape is obvious in comparing two boats alongside each other. On the left is the *Ripple*, SS19, and on the right is *Snowdrop*, built in Porthleven in 1925. Note the side propellers.

> The east Cornish lugger *Our Boys*, FY221, sailing in 2010. Built by Dick Pearce of East Looe in 1904, she is typical of these boats and is one of many that have survived and are still sailing today, albeit as pleasure craft.

it is regarded by many as trawling. Each seine was operated by a seine company – there were lots of these companies in Cornwall – and each had at least three boats, the largest being the seiner, an open boat rowed by at least six men and up to 40ft in length. The next, slightly smaller, was the stop-seine boat, sometimes called the folyer, aboard which was the net. The third was the lurker, which was much smaller and carried the Master Seiner: the man in charge of the whole process.

Crabbers also worked from many of the beaches along the south coast, such as Gorran Haven, Portloe, Coverack, Cadgwith and Sennen Cove. On the north coast of Cornwall, smaller luggers worked out of smaller places such as Port Isaac. In the river Fal, the Falmouth working boat remains unique in Britain as being the only fishing boat required by law to work under sail – in their case, when they are towing their oyster dredges in the confines of the river.

BRISTOL CHANNEL

The Bristol Channel – and here we will take its geographical limits as Hartland Point in Devon and across to St Govan's Head in Pembrokeshire – is not especially renowned for its vast fish stocks. Having said that, herring was an important species in the wide reaches. Herring spawn along parts of the Devon and Somerset coasts,

as well as off parts of Pembrokeshire, and healthy fisheries have been long established at places such as Clovelly, Minehead and Tenby.

Clovelly's herring fishery goes back centuries, and is probably older than its pier, which was first built in the fourteenth century. Centuries later, Clovelly herring boats were heavy, transom-sterned lug-rigged, half-deckers, though they probably had been square-sailed. In the late 1880s the fishermen turned to a lighter but similarly rigged type that enabled them to get to sea quicker than was possible with the older heavier boats, the Bristol Channel having the second largest tidal range in the world. These smaller boats became known as picarooners (sea robbers/

◀ Because the herring boats were heavy craft, the fishermen adopted the small picarooner to get fishing quicker from the tidal harbour. This replica vessel, *Little Lily*, seen sailing here in 2008, is used for herring drifting each autumn. (Courtesy of Simon & Ann Cooper)

◀◀ Clovelly, on the north coast of Devon, has had a small fishing fleet for centuries, mostly catching herring in autumn and potting in summer. These herring boats were the mainstay of the fleet.

pirates in Spanish) as the older fishermen regarded them as robbing them of their catch. They were lug-rigged with a large dipping lug mainsail and much smaller standing lug mizzen. They were renowned for having an extremely pretty 'wine glass' transom. Similar boats worked along the coast at nearby Bucks Mills, and from Ilfracombe, Lynmouth and Minehead. Long-boomers were smack-rigged trawlers with a long overhanging main boom that were in fact ubiquitous all along the coast.

Watchet had a fleet of sea-going flatners, which were a development of the boats of the Somerset levels. They were flat-bottomed and cheap to produce, and had centreboards for stability. Weston-super-Mare also had a few clinker-built flatners that, although sharing the same name and sprit rig, were quite dissimilar in hull shape.

Across the Channel, Mumbles oyster skiffs worked from Swansea and Mumbles, these being open oared boats until the east coast boats arrived, at which time the locals adopted the smack-rigged craft. Clinker-built Tenby luggers worked drift nets, trawls and oyster dredges from the town that was once the most important fish town in Wales. These were rigged in the same way as the Clovelly boats except some set a sprit mizzen and were as heavily built as the original herring boats, with a cuddy beneath the foredeck.

➤➤ Tenby, across the Bristol Channel, was once the greatest fishing station in the whole of Wales. Here a fleet of the small Tenby luggers are lined up on the beach, propped up on legs. Many have engines with wide cut-outs in the rudder to accommodate the propeller.

WEST WALES & NORTH-WEST ENGLAND

Cardigan Bay had several small fishing communities along its exposed coast. Small double-ended and transom-sterned beach boats served these communities. One of the most extraordinary of these was the three-masted Aberystwyth boat with its three narrow sails, the two forward masts of equal height having gaff sails on very short gaffs and a sprit mizzen. Aberporth was an important herring station in the eighteenth century and heavily built boats worked close to the shore. Similar herring boats worked from Cardigan and St Dogmaels, though, unlike Aberporth where they launched off the beach, these latter boats were moored in the river.

Off the Llyn peninsula, although herring was a seasonal fishery, lobsters were plentiful. Double-enders chased herring, as well as serving the off-lying Bardsey Island. Aberdaron, a small village at the end of the peninsula, still today retains a small fleet of Aberdaron fishing boats, which adopted the transom to ease the hauling of the pots, although they do not fish any longer, but simply race in the summer months.

Anglesey had its own beach boats, lug rigged with, often, a small triangular mizzen. Fishing all along this coast was more of a

◄ A fleet of round-sterned Morecambe Bay prawners on the end of Southport pier in 1897. These craft, more used to fishing for prawns, nevertheless were ready for a busy bank holiday weekend taking trips out around the bay. The design is unique to the area and evolved from early smacks through a transformation to suit the local conditions of the bay, with refinement from the naval architect William Stoba.

part-time occupation, for there was plenty of work ashore on the farms or at slate quarries. Welsh seamen also sailed the oceans aboard Welsh-built ships, although it was usual for them to return home for herring season as it was said a man could earn as much during the herring season as he earned the rest of the year.

The boat that served the offshore Welsh fleet was what was generally known as a Morecambe Bay nobby, a boat originating from the Lancashire coast but the use of which spread down as far as Cardigan Bay. I have heard them referred to as Welsh nobbies, and some were built in Conwy, but the majority were from further north. The nobbies – sometimes referred to as Lancashire nobbies and Morecambe Bay prawners – worked trawls for shrimp, prawns and flatfish, as well as whitefish in deeper water.

DID YOU KNOW?

One hundred and seventy-eight smacks were sunk by U-boats surfacing and scuttling them after setting many of the crews adrift in small boats during the First World War.

THE ISLE OF MAN

Across the sea, the Isle of Man has had a rich fishing culture going back centuries. The earliest boats there the scowtes, which were similar to the double-enders of Scotland and were Norse-influenced. These weren't the most seaworthy of craft and, after a particular storm wiped out much of the fleet in 1787, the Manxmen adopted smacks for fishing. However, seeing Scottish and Cornish luggers fishing their waters, they changed to a lug rig. In time they chose to swap to the lugger hull, these being named nickeys, after, it is said, the number of Cornishmen called Nicholas!

These were two-masted powerful luggers that were eventually larger than the Cornish boats. However, when the Loch Fyne fishers changed over to their half-decked skiffs in the 1880s, the Manx herring fishers

▲ The Manxmen were so impressed with the luggers from, mostly, Cornwall that they adopted the design in their nickeys, one of which is seen here leaving Peel harbour.

⌃ As the cost of building and crewing large vessels increased, many Manx fishers adopted a vessel similar to the ringnetters of Loch Fyne and so evolved the Manx nobby, a shortened, lugrigged version of the nickey, with a sloping sternpost to aid manoeuvrability. (Courtesy of Tom Cashin)

copied the design and so evolved the Manx nobby, which in no way reflected those nobbies from the mainland. In Ramsey they tended to fish long-lines and trawls, and an early vessel was said to be the Manx baulk yawl, a square-sailed open boat. However, the fishers here eventually adopted a boat very similar to the Lancashire nobbies.

IRELAND

Ireland's fishery was under British control until the early twentieth century, so unsurprisingly, many of the craft are similar to British patterns. Around the north coast, the drontheim was an obvious Scandinavian-influenced vessel, again similar to many Scottish boats. Further south they called them yawls or skiffs. On the County Down coast, the fishermen brought in Cornish and Manx craft, particularly favouring the Manx nickeys and, later, the Manx nobbies. On the west coast, Zulus on the Scottish design were brought in, albeit smaller at about 50ft, and mostly financed by the Congested Districts Board, a government department formed to invigorate the fisheries. Individual types evolved around the south coast, the most notable being the

◄◄ In the north of the island, the Ramsey boats tended to adhere to the Morecambe Bay shape, here seen in *Master Frank*, built in 1895. (Courtesy of Mike Craine)

◄ The Scottish-built small Zulu *Leenan Head*, built in 1909 with funding from the Congested Districts Board, was typical of many of the larger fishing boats from the Donegal coast. This boat has been restored and still sails under French ownership.

Towelsail yawls of Roaringwater Bay. Sea-going skin currachs (*naomhog*) fished around the south-west peninsulas. Other vessels of note are the Achill yawls, the West Cork mackerel yawls, the Loughbeg shrimp boats and the Arklow yawls.

◄ Ardglass, Northern Ireland, with nobbies very similar to those from the Isle of Man. The two both nearest the camera are Scottish fifies.

▲ In the south-west of Ireland lobster boats worked in Roaringwater Bay. They were renowned for remaining fishing for days on end and became known as Towelsail yawls from their habit of using the sail to form a tent, under which the crew would sleep.

Steam power might have been one of the most important developments in Britain's Industrial Revolution, which began in the eighteenth century, but it wasn't until the next century that it had any effect upon the fishing fleets. Indeed, even if steam was used to power moving engines in the latter part of the eighteenth century, it wasn't until about 1815 that the first boat was powered by steam. British fishermen had to wait another forty years or so to benefit, and that was only for steam-powered paddle tugs to tow their sailing boats out to sea, dropping them off just beyond the harbour limits. It was not until 1877 that William Purdy of North Shields decided to use his tug *Messenger* as a trawler without the need for a smack. Fishermen looked on in incredulity at the stupidity of such a thing – not for the first time were the fishermen adverse to any change. They generally regarded this 'absurdly new-fangled and impractical' idea a total waste of time and money. But when Purdy gained good results after two trips out, even realising a good profit, it didn't take long for the non-believers to copy his way.

Thus an enterprising vessel owner launched a purpose-built steam trawler. The *Zodiac*, launched in 1881, was owned by the Great Grimsby Steam Trawling Company, and it was immediately successful in that its catches were at least four times

1,000 steamers had been built in Britain. It was the same across Europe, where steam was impacting on, and superseding, traditional sailing boat types.

By the turn of the twentieth century a typical steam trawler was 120ft in length and 20ft in beam. Each had a triple-expansion engine of some 50–60hp that was situated aft in the boat. By 1909 there were 1,336 based in England and Wales (514 in Grimsby and 449 at Hull), and another 278 in Scotland, mostly working out of Aberdeen.

It was a different story for the drift-net fisheries. The fishermen believed that the size and noise from the steam engine frightened away the herring when they were drifting to their nets,

◀◀ The port of Banff, on the Moray Firth, with a mixture of sailing and steam fishing boats. The original steam drifters were simply larger fifies but the design soon changed into the wonderfully evocative low freeboarders.

greater than the average smack's. Even taking into account that she burned 4 tons of coal a day and had cost possibly three times as much as a smack, she was still more profitable. Within ten years of Purdy's experiments, an incredible

➤ Steamers jostling for quayside space in Lowestoft. The numbers of steamers built – both trawlers and drifters – was simply massive and, sadly, only a very few have survived through time, probably due to the cost of upkeep and running.

and so kept to their sailing luggers. The cost was also prohibitive and it wasn't until 1897 that the first steam drifter was launched. *Consolation*, LT718, was built by Chambers & Colby and looked much like any smack except for its tall funnel. Soon more appeared, looking more like the steam trawler, although they were lower in freeboard for hauling nets over, and wooden hulls were preferred to begin with until riveted iron gained favour. Lengths were up to 90ft and they were renowned

DID YOU KNOW?

Crews slept in the front part of a steam drifter where a man asleep in his bunk might rise 10ft up as the bow of the boat sailed up a wave, only to drop 10ft vertically downwards as the bow plunged over the wave.

◄ Steel soon out-dated wood for the larger steamers such as *Justifier*, LT224, sailing into port.

for their tall funnel, which led to the nicknames of either 'Woodbines' or 'Pipe-stalkies'.

During the First World War almost 3,000 steam trawlers and drifters were requisitioned by the Admiralty for mine-sweeping and patrol duties, and almost 400 were sunk on naval duty, with 2,058 fishermen's lives lost. After the war, with changing trends in motive power, their numbers quickly declined. Even by 1939 over 1,000 mostly steam trawlers were requisitioned, although many of these had had their steam engines removed and replaced by diesel motors. After the war the survivors gradually disappeared so that only a few remain today. The best known is probably the Great Yarmouth-based *Lydia Eva*, YH89, built in 1930.

DID YOU KNOW?

During the First World War there were 1,502 steam drifters and 1,467 steam trawlers requisitioned for minesweeping and patrol duties. Three hundred and ninety-four were lost during service whilst another 675 boats were sunk while fishing.

◄ In a very different way, the *Pioneer*, PZ277, was a steam-driven vessel built on the beach at St Ives by renowned boatbuilder William Paynter in 1899. She was originally only 35ft and one of several counter-sterner luggers built, but was lengthened to 47ft and later re-engined. Today she has been restored and is based in Hayle. (Courtesy of Jim Richards)

The idea of putting an internal combustion engine into a fishing boat appears to have first occurred in Denmark in 1895 when a Mollerup engine was installed into a fishing boat in Esbjerg. Various other experiments occurred in Norway and Holland but it wasn't until 1901 that the first British vessel thus powered arrived on the scene. Surprisingly, it was a new boat rather than simply an engine installed into an existing vessel; the suitably named *Pioneer*, LT368, was built by Henry Reynolds in his yard at Oulton Broad, Lowestoft, and looked much like any smack, with its rig. The engine was an American 38hp four-cylinder Globe Marine gasoline engine from Philadelphia. Within a couple of years she produced some startling results, much to the chagrin of the fishermen who again distrusted such innovation.

It was the same in Scotland where, in 1905, a new build was fitted with a 25hp Dan engine which the Fishery Board had recommended. The boat, also named *Pioneer* and registered ML30, was built in Anstruther and appeared like any fifie. She was regarded as an underpowered slow boat but her first year's fishing was met with some success. At the same time other fishermen were having engines put into their vessels, both new and old. One Sheringham open beach boat, the whelker *Reaper*, YH34, had an early M-type Gardner paraffin engine fitted, which produced

LLARY FISHING YAWL FITTED WITH FAIRBANKS MOTOR AT STROMNESS.

◄ An Orkney yole in Stromness as an early motor conversion, c.1910. (Photo courtesy Orkney Photo Archive)

>> The motorised Zulu *Smiling*, BF772, built in 1902 and later motorised and seen here before 1918 when her name was changed to *Blighty*. She survived, albeit with more name changes, until being broken up in 1953.

amazing results. By 1907 Henry Reynolds, who was still busy building steam drifters, had fitted a 60hp Brauer & Betts engine into *Thankful*, LT1035. In Ireland, the first motor-driven fishing boat, *Avoca*, was built by Tyrrell & Sons of Arklow in 1908, financed by the Fisheries Department of the Board of Agriculture.

DID YOU KNOW?

If all the nets from all the British fishing boats drift-netting for herring in 1900 were joined up, they would reach across the Atlantic Ocean.

EAST COAST OF SCOTLAND

It wasn't until the Scottish 1901-built fifie *Maggie Jane*, BK145, had a 55hp Gardner fitted in 1907 that the idea of motorising the fishing fleet gained a foothold, although the yard of J. & G. Forbes of Sandhaven had already built an experimental motorboat fitted with the very first Gardner engine, which was later fitted out with sails to save fuel. Several more conversions followed, such as, in 1908, the 50-ton fifie *Vineyard*. The following year it was the turn of the 48-ton Arbroath fifie *Ebenezer*, AH46, to have a 60hp Blackstone heavy oil engine fitted.

The first large vessel on the Moray Firth so engined was in fact a Zulu, the 42-ton, 1902-built *Mother's Joy*, BF892, which had a 60hp Fairbanks-Remington installed in 1909. On the other hand, the Zulu, with its steeply raking sternpost, was found largely unsuited to conversion, even if a few such as *Lady Hill*, INS522, were also motorised by cutting away huge chunks of the sternpost and in some cases adding a bit to alter the angle of rake. Generally, whereas motor fifies continued to be built, no new Zulus were manufactured after this time. However, those fifies built were

▲ The motor fifie *Chrysolite*, ML237, seen entering the river Yare c.1930. Low down in the water, she has a good catch of herring aboard.

▼ The Danish type of seine-net boat proved successful in some east coast ports and here is the Grimsby registered *Margit*. These vessels became known as 'snibbies' by many, because of their cut-off shape. (Courtesy of Malcolm Cook)

generally smaller than their large counterparts as it was soon realised that smaller boats needed smaller engines, which were cheaper to fit and run.

The First World War prevented further motorisation and fishing itself was severely restricted.

Although the peak of the herring fishery was in 1913, war meant it collapsed the following year through the loss of the Russian and Eastern European markets, and it never regained momentum after the Armistice in 1918. But, within a couple of years, stories of new methods of fishing from across the other side of the North Sea were reaching the fishermen's ears.

This was the Danish seine method which, although its use dates back to the mid 1800s, attracted the attention of British fishermen when the Danes started fishing on the west side of the North Sea after the war. Some skippers started using the same gear aboard their herring drifters and steam trawlers.

In Scotland, the first time it was used was in 1921. They elaborated the Danish way into what became known as 'fly-dragging'.

Both steam-powered and motorised boats were working the Danish seine-net. The Danes were fishing with their cruiser-sterned boats – shark cutters, they called them – but, although the fishermen would have liked to build similar vessels, they couldn't afford them. For boatbuilding, times were hard and yards either went out of business or temporarily closed while others had to hunt around for whatever work they could get. The Forbes yard, for example, did close but reopened in 1925.

In 1928 the first boat to be designed specifically for the Danish seine was the 50ft *Marigold*, built by William Wood & Sons of Lossiemouth. Although these new hulls slightly increased in volume, and the sternpost tended to rake to somewhere around 10–20 degrees,

◀◀ Peterhead harbour, 1920s, with early motorised vessels and a steam drifter in the background. This was a period of change, both in design of vessel and mode of fishing. The two nearest boats were working the Danish seine net, judging by the coils of rope.

>> By the late 1940s the east coast yards were building cruiser- and canoe-sterned vessels. Here the Walter Reekie-built *Achates*, LH232, dating from 1949, is seen leaving Peel harbour. Built for the ring-net with larch planking on oak frames and low bulwarks, the boat was based at Fisherrow, near Edinburgh, but fished the west coast herring.

to the untrained eye there was little difference immediately obvious in the design of the new boats. The old sailing fifie just became the motor fifie, though they began to be referred to as motor seiners, and have also been erroneously termed half-Zulus. *Marigold* was fitted with a 36hp Gardner semi-diesel engine and was found to be very economical in comparison to the steam drifters.

This period saw an upsurge in business for the Scottish yards, as they were building these seiners just as the method overtook herring drifting. These same yards supplied boats down the coast, to harbours such as Whitby. Different yards had different attitudes to shape, and two boats that looked pretty much the same from the bow might have differing angles of the sternpost.

In and around Fraserburgh, small motorised yoles became a favourite

DID YOU KNOW?

Many fishermen were slow to accept change – when engines first appeared they sceptically referred to these things as 'new-fangled ideas that would never catch on'.

▲ A small Fraserburgh yole, *Restless Wave*, FR2. These vessels generally were built for the sma' line fishing, i.e. fishing inshore with long lines.

responsible for changing the whole face of fishing-boat design. This was the construction of the first Scottish-built cruiser-sterned boat, *Cutty Sark*, which was obviously influenced by the Danish boats, although with a straight stem rather than the typical rounded Danish one. However, until the introduction of the transom stern, the cruiser stern was to become the staple design for what became known as the Scottish motorised fishing vessel (MFV), later adopted by the Admiralty. Interestingly, *Cutty Sark* was not a successful boat – at 45ft, she was probably a bit small. Larger boats came next, including the dual-purpose *Gleanaway*, KY40, in 1929 and *Efficient*, FR242, in 1931.

amongst the inshore fishermen. Most of these were built by James Nobles of Fraserburgh, J. & G. Forbes or Tommy Summers.

The year 1928 also saw a new build that eventually was

◄ The vessel on the right is the *Comely III*, based in Pittenweem, a typical transomed vessel used for creeling for lobsters and crabs. The vessel alongside is rigged for trawling, and the *Comely III* can also be set up to trawl and is called a 'dual-purpose' boat.

➤ The motorised fifie *Brighter Dawn*, KY656, has a steam capstan situated abaft the mainmast. These capstans revolutionised fishing as for the first time manpower for hauling was at a minimum. Coupled with the loss of sails, crews decreased in number.

Gleanaway is often referred to as the first true Scottish fishing vessel built with a cruiser stern and at 75ft, powered by a 140hp Fairbanks Morse engine, she certainly was the first successful one, even if *Cutty Sark* was built a year earlier.

Much as hull shape dictated the pace of change, so did the wheelhouse building. From the early pillbox tiny affairs to deck-house accommodation with their raised bridge decks, these structures were just as fundamental to the beauty of these wooden fishing craft.

There were other factors that dictated boat development such as the introduction of lighter cotton nets from the older heavy hemp nets, thus allowing more nets to be shot. Hauling in nets was also made easier with capstans, the hand-worked Iron Man being commonplace aboard the large luggers. Elliott & Garrood produced their first steam capstan about 1884 and these were in general use aboard boats by 1895. Motorisation led to the development of winches and haulers, powered directly by the engine.

WEST COAST OF SCOTLAND

On the west coast of Scotland it was a different story. The Lochfyne skiff *Brothers*, CN97, owned by fisherman Robert Robertson, was the first to have an engine installed in 1907, this being a Kelvin 7.9hp petrol/paraffin motor from the Glasgow manufacturer. Later that year another Lochfyne skiff, *Lady Carrick Buchanan*, CN38, had a 7.5hp Thornycroft paraffin motor fitted. By the end of that year there were at least ten engined boats working the west coast. However, because of the configuration of the raked sternpost – although not as steeply sloping as the Zulus – the propeller shafts were led out on the starboard side through a fashioned strengthening piece of wood. This was because the nets were always set and hauled on the port side and the prop wouldn't then foul the net.

In 1908 the skiff *Ellen*, CN95, was also engined by Kelvin engineers at Hunters Quay. A succession of conversions continued over the next few years. By 1912 new skiffs were still being built and engines were being installed as part of the contract. One of these was their 40ft skiff *Perseverance*, CN152, built by Robert Wylie at Campbeltown, which had a larger 13.15hp Kelvin poppet-valve engine fitted. She neighboured the *Ellen* at the ring-net when boats worked in pairs. Over her working

➤➤ The Lochfyne skiff *Ella* raising anchor. The boat is motorised and, although the mast has been retained, there are no sails visible. Many west coast fishermen favoured Kelvin engines, manufactured in Glasgow by the Bergius Launch & Engine Company. (Courtesy of Margaret McBride Harvison)

life from Campbeltown, which lasted until 1946, she had three different Kelvins installed, each one of a slightly improved design.

Use of the Lochfyne skiffs continued through the 1910s and the fleet expanded with new vessels. Only in a few instances did the fishermen favour the east coast types of vessel until, in 1922, the design of boat altered considerably. This change was due to one fisherman, the aforementioned Robert Robertson who is highly regarded as an innovative fisherman who developed the efficiency of the ring-net and boat design. His Norwegian design-inspired new boat came from the drawing board of Glasgow naval architect W.G. McBride after he had been asked by Robertson to design a vessel with a canoe stern. This resulted in two new boats Robertson invested in, the *Falcon* and the *Frigate Bird*, built by James Miller of St Monans, arriving in Campbeltown in April 1922 to begin work. Of course the rest of the fishermen were astonished that he could waste his money on vessels that were totally different to what they were used to. There were a few similarities to the skiffs: low freeboard, forward accommodation and a rig, but there it stopped. They were 50ft in length, fully decked and the forefoot was cut away to facilitate steerage, necessary when operating a ring-net in confined waters. Each boat also had two

> ## DID YOU KNOW?
>
> The first engines were so unreliable that the fishermen retained their rigs for when the engines broke down.

Gleniffer 18–22hp engines. Soon the boats proved their worth, increasing catches and profitability.

In 1930 Robertson sold his original two boats and had built two new 52ft boats, *Kestrel* and *Kittiwake*. By this time a transom-sterned boat, the *Unitas* from Saltcoats, was adapted by having a canoe stern built on, the first Ayrshire boat to have such an arrangement. By 1933, thirteen new boats, all built on the east coast of Scotland from the yards of J. Miller, Walter Reekie of St Monans, Weatherhead & Blackie of Cockenzie (previously William Weatherhead worked alone) and James Noble of Fraserburgh, were introduced into the Campbeltown and Carradale fleets, while fourteen

➤ The *Falcon*, the first of the new breed of boats to work the ring-net on the west coast. Retaining the lugsail, but having both a canoe stern and a wheelhouse, this boat arrived in 1922, much to the astonishment of the fishermen. However, it didn't take long for the design to catch on, and the older skiffs soon disappeared. (Courtesy of Angus Martin)

Girvan soon after the Second World War he built, over a period of some thirty years, some of their finest ringers. Not surprising then that these ringers, with their varnished hulls, pretty sheer lines and canoe sterns, added to the mystique surrounding the ring-net and remain centremost in many a west coast man's heart.

were added to the Ayrshire fleet at Dunure, Girvan and Ballantrae. The design had finally found favour and the demise of the older Lochfyne skiffs was now a certainty. Over the next few years many more motor ring-netters were built before war intervened once again. When Alexander Noble opened his yard in

DID YOU KNOW?

The 'Kipper patrol' was a fleet of fishing boats that defended the British coast during the Second World War.

Three ringers at Caradale: *Shemaron*, CN244, *Fair Maid*, CN248, and *Bairn's Pride*, BA125. *Shemaron*, built by Nobles of Girvan in 1949, still sails as a private boat, one of only a handful of these fine boats to have survived. *Fair Maid* was built by Weatherhead of Eyemouth, also in 1949 whilst *Bairn's Pride* came from Millers of St Monans in 1948. (Courtesy of Finlay Oman)

CORNWALL

Like the west coast of Scotland, it wasn't until 1907 that motors began to be fitted into Cornish vessels, although they had already been affected after some luggers had had steam capstans fitted years before, replacing the earlier flywheel capstans. But it was only then that they adopted motors to propel their boats. Once the initial suspicion had dissipated, it was found that the luggers – especially the transomed ones from the east – were relatively easy to convert.

However, this didn't stop those from the west. In St Ives, for example, the first boats engined were the *Gleaner*, SS123, and *Family*, SS61, in 1910. During the First World War many more were motorised through finances advanced from the Motor Loans Committee of the Ministry of Agriculture, Fisheries

◄◄ The *Crystal Sea*, OB104, was slightly largely than *Village Maid II* at just over 60ft and came from the Girvan yard. Both these boats continued fishing until they were decommissioned in the 1990s.

◄ St Ives around 1940 with a small gig on the left (*May*, SS47) and the motor lugger *Francis Stevens*, SS49, with drift-nets on the deck. Note the centre line and side propellers – it was normal in Cornwall to have at least two engines, often situated forward in the boat. (Courtesy of John McWilliams)

and Food. Many were fitted with Kelvin engines from Glasgow, which proved popular in the county over the next few decades, so much so that Cornwall had several Kelvin agents. Within two decades the transition was complete: in 1923 there was one sail boat left in Fowey and fifty-seven motorboats, of which thirty-one had been one-time sailing luggers. The story was the same in the west of Cornwall where, in 1930, there were thirty-four motorboats registered at Penzance and twenty-five at St Ives.

Cornish boats usually had two engines, the main one on the centre line for reaching the fishing grounds and another smaller unit on the starboard side for working the nets.

DID YOU KNOW?

Harry Tate (real name Ronald Macdonald Hutchinson) was a music hall comedian between the world wars. He was renowned for poking fun at the navy and, due to the dilapidated state of much of the fishing fleet from the requisitioning of 1939, they became known as Harry Tate's Navy!

This was set at an angle to the centre line so that the shaft passed over the main shaft and protruded out on the port side. The nets were always set and hauled over the starboard side thus the propeller was kept clear on the port side. Some boats such as the *Lindy Lou*, FY382, had three engines, the third one driving a winch to haul in the long-lines. Engines were usually situated forward so that the accommodation was retained at the after end, unlike most of the Scottish boats which either had the accommodation at the forward, uncomfortable, end or amidships. Having the engine forward necessitated having a long shaft running almost two-thirds of the length of the boat.

◄ The *Coeur de Lion*, PZ74, was built by Nobles of Fraserburgh in 1957 for Dick Sampson of Newlyn and was one of the last Cornish boats ring-netting off the Irish coast in 1961. She is seen here in about 1978 moored at the back of the north quay of Custom House Quay in Falmouth, from where she was working at the pilchards and other fisheries. (Courtesy of Luke Powell)

THE HARBOUR, FOLKESTONE

⌃ Another boat to escape being chopped up on decommissioning is the *Happy Return*, FE5, which was built by Kitto of Porthleven in 1905. Many of the Folkestone fishermen favoured the Cornish luggers and *Happy Return* was by no means the only one working the Kent coast. She was restored in the early part of this century and is based in Penzance. (Courtesy of William Gale)

▲ The *Lindy Lou*, FY382, was built as a mackerel drifting and long-lining boat by Curtis and Pape of Looe in 1947. She's fuller than the sailing luggers, and originally had two engines from new. She was decommissioned in 1998 and was one of a few boats that escaped the chainsaw, thanks largely to the work of the 40+ Fishing Boat Association. (Courtesy of John McWilliams)

◀ In Ireland, the first purpose-built motorboat was the 48ft *Avoca*, built by Tyrrells of Arklow and launched in 1908. Motorisation had the same effects on the fishing industry, with support given by government by way of grants to build new boats. The photo shows the *Ros Ailither*, D428, built by the BIM yard in Killybegs in 1954 and seen here in Brest in 2016. She fished from Wexford and then the Aran Islands, before ending up at Looe in the 1990s as FY518, and eventually being converted for pleasure and transatlantic sailing.

So we've seen how what is often referred to as the Scottish MFV evolved through influence from Norway and how, not for the first time, Scandinavian characteristics had been built into British fishing vessel design. During the 1930s a whole host of cruiser-sterned boats were built, although it has to be remembered that new small inshore craft continued to run down the slipways of the yards. Even the motorised fifies continued to be built until 1938, the last one regarded as being *Dorothy*, GY545, built by A. Aitken of Anstruther for Grimsby owners. At almost 49ft, she was typical of sixteen of these vessels that Aitken had built over a seven-year period. In general, during the period between the end of the war in 1945 and the 1970s, Scotland produced some of the finest and longest-serving fishing boats in the world. Their use spread far and wide around Britain as the older sailing designs disappeared. One of the most prolific and respected Scottish builders of these boats was Richard Irvin of Peterhead who, between 1953 and 1978, built fifty wooden-hulled MFVs over 70ft in length. To emphasise what is written in the Introduction, Gloria Wilson, that doyen of Scottish fishing boats, once wrote that Irvin's boats were based 'more on art, intuition and personal opinion than on the science of naval architecture'.

◀ Two boats at Maryport. *Sincerity*, LH188, was built by Richard Irvin of Peterhead in 1962 and is seen here with trawling gear in 2003. *Islander*, BA316, on the other hand, is a west coast boat coming from Nobles of Girvan, built as *Islesman* in 1967 for Isle of Lewis owners.

> The traditional wooden MFV cannot get much better in appearance than vessels such as *Crimond*, BCK118. Built by the Berthon Boat Company of Lymington as an Admiralty MFV (No. 1225) in 1946, she was sold as a herring drifter the following year and renamed *Elm*. Here she is in the early 1960s coming into Ullapool. The Admiralty built hundreds of boats to use during wartime, the intention being to sell them off after hostilities to the fishing industry both to invigorate fishing and off-load its stock of vessels. (Courtesy of Peter Lambie)

In Cornwall, several of the established boatbuilders built canoe- and cruiser-sterned boats for the local fisheries, a good example being the canoe-sterned *Sweet Promise*, SS95, built by Percy Mitchell of Porthmellon

DID YOU KNOW?

Admiralty MFVs were vessels built under orders from, and financed by, the Admiralty during periods of war. They were used for naval duty and were then sold off after hostilities to benefit the fishing industry. Today many have survived and have been converted for pleasure use or further work.

The lovely varnished hull of *Florae*, A56, coming into Aberdeen soon after her launch at Gerrard's Yard, Arbroath, in 1955. The Torry Fishery Research Station is in the background.

and launched in 1953. Curtis and Pape (previously known as Curtis & Mitchell before Alan Pape joined after the Second World War) built several from their yard in West Looe.

Cornwall and Devon were also home to fleets of beam trawlers, steel boats often built in Holland that used beam trawls set on outriggers to trawl along the sea bottom. These are medium-sized and high-powered vessels to counteract the drag of the heavy beams, and this method of fishing is regarded as being one of the most destructive because of the damage to the seabed.

As diesel engines developed, power take-offs allowed belt-driven winches and rope coilers to aid the work on deck, as we saw in the last chapter. During the period between the 1930s and 1965, Kelvin and Gardner engines were used almost universally aboard fishing boats, especially Scottish-built ones. Then came hydraulics in the 1960s, which allowed power blocks (the Puretic power block, a mechanised drum winch, was actually invented in Croatia in 1953) and rope reels to increase the hauling ability.

➤ Beam trawlers at Brixham, 2016. These steel boats run two beam trawls, one either side, and the size of the trawl can be seen here. Boats such as these also work in the Channel from Newlyn, as well as the Dutch having a fleet. They have very powerful engines to drag such large trawls.

Also in the 1960s, the transom stern was introduced into the offshore fleet, soon replacing the double ender. The transom gave added buoyancy aft, necessary for the increasing size of engine. It also produced more deck space for the ever-growing winches, the ability to trawl over the stern and more room below for accommodation. The downside was that it gave inferior sea-keeping qualities in following seas and also reduced speed, with there being greater drag beneath a transom. Whatever the personal opinion, Irvin never built a transom-sterned vessel as many of the seine-net fishermen preferred the cruiser stern. This prevailed until 1986, when the last

DID YOU KNOW?

The fishing boat *Girl Pat*, GY176, built in Lowestoft in 1935, made headlines in 1936 when its skipper Dod Orsborne and his crew sailed her to Georgetown, British Guiana, without the owners' permission, using only a sixpenny school atlas and a compass. Orsborne was arrested, sent back to Britain and imprisoned after being found guilty. He maintained he'd been instructed to lose the boat for an insurance claim yet, years later, he suggested he was working for British Naval Intelligence. The boat later returned to the UK and was briefly requisitioned during the war.

two cruiser-sterned boats were built in Scotland: *Moray Endurance*, BCK34, and *Tyleana*, BF61, the latter working as a pair-trawler along with *Reliant*. This method of fishing allowed a larger net to be operated, with a wider mouth which was kept apart by the two boats sailing parallel to each other, whereas previously the mouth was held open using otter boards. *Tyleana* had a shelter covering most of her deck from aft of the wheelhouse to the bow – the so-called three-quarter shelter deck. This became a standard characteristic and was regarded as much a safety aspect as anything else, even if, in many people's minds, they lack any charm. In time, full-length shelter decks became almost standard as designs changed, often built in aluminium to reduce weight above the waterline. At the same time steel hulls built to standard specifications became the norm. Wooden boats almost died out, although both Macduff

◀◀ The *Alex Watt*, INS163, built in Banff in 1964, fished out of Lossiemouth for a number of years. The side shelter deck is an addition and the boat is obviously a trawler because of the two otter boards at the rear. The power block to haul in the net is also a later addition.

◀ The transom-sterned *Coquet Herald*, LH94, sailing in Loch Broom in 2016. She was built in Amble in 1974. Note the side shelter and whaleback – innovations when she was built. (Courtesy of Finlay Oman)

Shipyards of Macduff (they built their first steel boat in 1989 when they were the Macduff Boatbuilding & Engineering Co.) and C. Toms & Sons of Polruan, Cornwall, continued in the traditional vein. Tim Loftus, working in Bristol, also built the wooden 24ft dual-purpose trawler/creel boat *Girl Lauren* for Cockenzie owners, based on boats he'd seen on the west coast of Scotland. Nevertheless, the days of the beautiful lines of wooden fishing boats were over, and more standardised, almost prefabricated, boats became the order of the day.

Fibreglass also changed the face of wooden boatbuilding in that moulded hulls could be produced fairly quickly which, in turn, reduced the price. The disadvantage was that many of the boats looked the same and the days of the individuality of wooden vessels had gone. The ubiquitous fishing boat spread far and wide, both in the small inshore sector and offshore. Standardisation was the name of the game and, in terms of cost, this was good news.

➤ The steel *Arcturus*, UL88, built by Eyemouth Boatbuilding Company Ltd in 1985, is a very different shape to those we've seen up to now. The wheelhouse is set forward with plenty of space aft to bring in the trawl. Much of the working deck is covered, making life easier at sea.

Adele, BCK36, was one of the last wooden boats built by Macduff Shipyard in 2001. Even though the hull is wooden, the working deck is also entirely covered and the wheelhouse is amidships to give good visibility and plenty of space aft. (Courtesy of Bodies of Banff)

◄ *Provider*, AH71, leaving Oban in 2008. A product of Mackay Boatbuilders of Arbroath in 1972, she too has had the addition of a side shelter deck and whaleback. (Courtesy of Finlay Oman)

➤ Although her appearance might belie it, *Radiant Way*, KY151, seen here approaching the Skye Bridge in 2009, was built by Millers of St Monans in 1965. She's been heavily built over, and the wheelhouse looks almost buried under shelter decks. (Courtesy of Finlay Oman)

▲ *Village Belle IV*, TT74, is another boat from Nobles of Girvan, here seen in Oban, where she is based, in 2015. Built in 1970 as a ring-net boat, she now fishes for prawns and scallops and has none of the paraphernalia that many of the preceding boats have.

▲ *Guardian Angell*, LK272, was built by the Campbeltown Shipyard in 1992 for Orkney owners. At about 87ft in length, she has a full-length shelterdeck and is rigged for trawling. She is seen here in Whitby. (Courtesy of Carle Robinson)

◄ *Radiant*, ex-*Resplendent*, PD298, ashore in Peterhead in January 2002. The modern shape of fishing boats can be seen, with the bulbous bow, deep underwater section and forward wheelhouse with plenty of shelterdeck. She was built in Fraserburgh in 1981 and was sadly lost 45 miles off the Isle of Lewis in April of that year after the net snagged an underwater obstruction.

▼ The motorised coble *Laura Thurlow*, MH96, in 2016. It is common for the northern cobles to fix a cover over the forward part of the vessel to provide a degree of shelter. (Courtesy of Carle Robinson)

▲ The Northern Irish *Boys Pride*, N174, a modern efficient inshore fishing boat where the semi-displacement catamaran hulls are more fuel efficient than mono hulls. (Courtesy of Mike Craine)

▲ A photograph splendidly showing the new and old: on the left at Mallaig in 2001 is the 1972 Nobles of Girvan-built *Wanderer II*, CN142 (ex-*Aquila*, OB99), whilst the newer boat is the 1984 Macduff-built *Our Pride*, SH77. Both are wooden hulled though very different above water. (Courtesy of Edward Valentine)

In the main, these are the fishing boats that sailed far and wide in search of fish. Some of the earliest fishing ventures were off Newfoundland and New England in the late sixteenth century and onwards, and British ships – mostly from Devon and the West Country – sailed to follow the fishing for months at a time. However, these were sailing ships that were merely used as transport, setting out in the spring to set up accommodation on the shore. The men fished the inshore waters using hooks and lines aboard small boats to catch the cod, which was then cured ashore on stages and flakes (wooden drying platforms), and stored before they returned to Britain in the autumn.

However, the Icelandic and Faroese fisheries were at least a century older and, when John Cabot returned from his 'discovery' of Newfoundland, he reported cod the size of men and famously noted that there would be no need for the Icelandic fishery any longer! How wrong he was. By the end of the eighteenth century boats stopped fishing across the Atlantic and concentrated on fisheries a bit nearer to home.

Documented evidence of the boats sailing to Iceland and further north don't surface until the eighteenth century, when sailing smacks were departing from ports such as Harwich, where so-called cod smacks, or codbangers, were

◄ Fleetwood sailing trawlers – *Wonder*, FD68, and *Harriet*, FD111 – sailing out of the river Wyre at Fleetwood, beam trawls visible over their sterns.

successfully fishing there. In 1730 there were twenty-four such vessels, each with wet wells to keep the fish fresh. By the end of the century there were 100. By the mid 1800s, with the availability of ice, smacks from Aberdeen, Grimsby, Hull and Fleetwood headed for the Icelandic coast, fishing until their holds were full before making the passage home.

Fleetwood grew from what was little more than an uninhabited area around the estuary of the river Wyre in the beginning of the nineteenth century to a major fishery station in half a century.

The first Hull steam trawler sailed for Iceland in 1891 and made fantastic catches. The following year boats from other ports repeated the exercise and it was almost as if a bonanza had been realised. However, at the time Iceland was governed from Denmark (as were the Faroe Islands) and, not keen on the sudden influx of trawlers, in 1893 a 50-mile fishing limit was declared around its coast. However, this was not recognised and generally ignored by British trawler owners,

>> The motor drifter *Young Duke*, LT387, leaving Lowestoft en route to the herring fishing grounds. In the background are two steam drifters obviously heading the same way. Note the mizzen sails are up to steady the boats and the mainmast lowered in readiness to shoot the nets.

DID YOU KNOW?

The Total Allowable Catch (TAC) is the amount of a particular species of fish that can be caught in a certain ICES Statistical Area or groups of areas on a yearly or two-yearly basis under the European Common Fisheries Policy. Quota is the amount of TAC given to each country under a percentage rule.

the 1890s being regarded as 'El Dorado'. Danish gunboats patrolled the area and arrested several boats which were escorted into port and fined, with the catch confiscated. In 1896 an agreement was signed whereby British boats were able to shelter in Icelandic ports as long as they stowed their gear and nets, and didn't fish to the east of the country. Some arrests for so-called 'illegal fishing' still continued, although the outbreak of war in 1914 curtailed the fishing and no further agreements on the issue of Icelandic fishing were made.

During the late 1940s the design of the distant-water fleet altered drastically, due to the adoption of diesel engines. The very first of these 'oil burners' retained the old pipestalkie tall funnels and wheelhouse, though within a couple of years a more modest funnel and redesigned wheelhouse was adopted, giving the boat a more

➤ The stern view of the stern trawler *Jacinta*, FD159, described as perhaps the most famous of stern trawlers in the country. Built in 1972 on the river Tyne, she was soon breaking records and paid for herself in a short time. She continued to fish successfully from Hull until engine trouble caused her to be retired in 1994 and she was then taken back to Fleetwood to become a permanent maritime museum. Here she is in the Wyre Dock in 2009.

⌄ Here is a very different type of motor vessel, the side trawler *Boston Seahawk*, A178, registered in Aberdeen, another of the traditional distant water fishing ports. Built in Hessle in 1953 with a 500hp diesel engine, she was first registered in Lowestoft and then moved to Milford Haven before being sold to Aberdeen in 1957. She was re-engined with a Lister Blackstone 495hp diesel and in the 1970s worked from the west coast (Isle of Man, Fleetwood and Barmouth), being scrapped in 1986.

modern feel although the mizzen steadying sail continued to be part of the standard gear. Such a boat was the 178ft 1949-built *Cape Cleveland*, H61, owned by Hudson Brothers Trawlers Ltd. Built by John Lewis & Sons Ltd of Aberdeen, her name was changed in 1965 to *Ross Cleveland*, when Hudson's were taken over by the Ross Group. The hull form of these boats was considered to be the best for Arctic trawling. Sadly she was lost in appalling conditions in February 1968 with all but one of the crew perishing.

These boats were also called sidewinders because they set their trawls on one side of the vessel. Later boats had ramps in the stern so that they could haul their nets in there. These were called stern trawlers. Vessels continued fishing in Icelandic waters, even though subsequent 'Cod Wars' reduced their fishing ability right up to 1975. The last 'Cod War' saw Britain leaving these waters and the distant-water fishery became but a memory.

▲ Another Aberdeen side trawler, *Countesswells*, A366, is typical of the 1960s. Built in Aberdeen in 1960, she was sold to the fares in 1971 and renamed *Gullborg*. She sank soon after when the engine exploded; the crew were safely picked up.

When the *Efficient* was launched in 1931 in Fraserburgh, she was designed largely for herring fishing. However, although she served during the war years with the Admiralty, afterwards she moved to Newlyn, Cornwall. There she was first converted for trawling, then for gill-netting and in her final working days she was fishing for tuna in the Bay of Biscay. This merely shows that boats were then able to switch fisheries.

We've mentioned both steam trawlers and drifters, but several steamers were built specifically for lining and worked in the waters around the Northern Isles, Faroe and as far away as in Icelandic and Greenland waters. These 'great liners', as they were called, fished the grounds that the trawlers were unable to work over: the rocky deep waters. They set many fleets of lines, each up to 500 fathoms long with up to a 150 hooks fixed to snoods. During the war little great lining took place as single boats were not keen to venture out alone. For comparison, in 1943 great liners landed 4.1 per cent of the total Scottish white fish catch while seiners landed 31 per cent and trawlers 56.2 per cent, but within years there was a great revival after no fishing for several years. By 1948 there were twenty-two steam liners working out of Aberdeen and the percentage share of fish more than doubled. Two years later steam liners had swollen to thirty-four vessels, whilst there were another six motor liners by this time. Numbers then decreased over the next few years.

Anstruther, on the East Neuk of Fife, built four new motor liners in the 1950s: *Verbena*, KY97; *Silver Chord*, KY124; *Brighter Hope*, KY37; and *Radiation*, A115. The latter, at 97ft in length, was the largest liner built in Britain and was launched from the Smith & Hutton yard in Anstruther on 31 January 1957 in a force-10 storm. She was powered by a Mirrlees National TLSGMR6 engine. Built in wood, as it was thought that steel would double her cost, she principally fished for

▲ The herring boat *Excellent*, PZ513, originally built in Fraserburgh in 1931 as *Efficient* in 1947. She's been rigged for trawling, the A-frames for the trawl clearly seen either side of the mainmast. Note the small wheelhouse. Later she was adapted for gill-netting. (Courtesy of Billy Stevenson)

cod, skate, ling and halibut. She set forty-two fleets of lines, each 300 fathoms long with 100 hooks fixed to snoods on each. She fished throughout the 1960s when most remaining liners were either laid up or converted to trawling, and only ceased fishing in 1978, after which she went into museum ownership.

We've already seen how some sailing vessels were built for dredging oysters and collecting cockles. Scallop fishing became profitable in the twentieth century and boats were easily adapted to the fitting of dredges along the boat's sides. Boats were also built for dredging cockles and mussels.

On the east coast of Scotland the two East Neuk yards of J. Miller & Sons, St Monans, and Smith & Hutton, Anstruther, produced a series of fine double-ended motorised creel boats in the 1950s and 1960s. However, with the advent of fibreglass and the establishment of various transom-sterned models from reputable companies, these lovely wooden creel boats were generally short lived and became pleasure boats, even if a few survived in part-time use for fishing.

◄◄ The great line boat *Glenstruan*, A200, built in 1958 at Peterhead, was typical of the vessels that fished with lines off Iceland and Greenland. These boats stayed at sea for at least two weeks.

➤ Mussel dredger *Bonnie & Kelly*, N98. Built in west Wales in 1990, this boat dredged mussels, based in Port Penrhyn, Bangor, before being sold to Northern Ireland in the mid 1990s. She is basically a large open tank into which the mussels are dropped when dredged using the beams either side.

➤ A typical scallop dredger, the 1998-built *Sarah Lena*, CT18, a dual-purpose scalloper/trawler ensuring work throughout the year. (Courtesy of Mike Craine)

◄ Cockle dredgers at Annagassan in Dundalk Bay. The boat tows the suction dredge over the stern, pulling it along its skids. The flexible pipe allows the pump to bring the cockles up with sand whilst added seawater washes them clean through a sieve.

DID YOU KNOW?

Many hundreds of lives have been lost over a century of fishing and today fishing remains the most dangerous occupation undertaken by Britain's workforce.

Many of the creel boats – such as those just mentioned – can be grouped into what are termed inshore and river vessels. We've seen how varied fishing vessels that work in the offshore and deep-sea fishery have been over the decades, and the inshore and coastal fleet is probably even more diverse in its design. This group of vessels includes those that work directly off the beach, those that work in rivers and their estuaries, and many more small boats that undertake day fishing, such as creeling for lobsters and crabs. Any sheltered beach or small harbour will be full of such craft, although today few commercially fish and only a tiny minority will be traditionally built in wood.

One of the best examples of beach-based fisheries that still works is that of Hastings. Here quite a different motorised craft developed through the necessity of working directly off the beach. We saw the luggers of Hastings in Chapter 1, and the motorised vessels retained much of the same shape, though fuller bodied to stand upright. They had very rounded elliptical sterns, which coped well with the waves when coming onshore before being hauled up the beach. As to their size, they are today the largest beach craft working the British coast.

Many of the craft working off the beaches are open boats, once powered by sail or oar but now

with small engines installed, thus providing a more full-bodied shape. They are, these days, hauled up the beach by tractor. Sadly, many of the beaches where these boats once worked are now empty through legislation and lack of quota. Apart from Hastings, some – such as Aldeburgh in Suffolk and Cadgwith in Cornwall – do retain some beach activity, with their own type of regional motorised craft in work. The Clovelly picarooner, as mentioned in Chapter 1, is included in this group and one boat continues to fish today.

▲ Typical small lobster fibreglass boat at St Andrews in 2001.

◄ The beach-based fishing community at Cove, near Aberdeen, with small fifie yawls. (Courtesy of Edward Valentine)

Over the centuries, many British rivers and estuaries have seen healthy fisheries for such species as salmon, sea trout, eels, herring, trout and occasionally other fish. Salmon and eels have been the most profitable and some rivers have seen

DID YOU KNOW?

In some parts of Britain, such as Morecambe Bay, they used horses to tow trawls around in shallow water. These caught shrimps and prawns.

huge concentrations of fishing. But, as licences began to be issued in the late nineteenth century, these have, over the last fifty or so years, been determinedly withdrawn so that today few commercial fishermen are able to fish these waters.

⋀ The Grimsay lobster boat Lily in 2001.

◄◄ A typical clinker-built beach boat ashore at Red Wharf Bay, Anglesey.

In Scotland, salmon cobles were suited to these conditions: flat-bottomed to be beached easily and stable enough to work in the tidal estuaries. Their size decreased the further upstream they worked.

In England, various rivers were worked. In the West Country, rivers such as the Exe, the Torridge and the Taw had their own salmon boats, small open craft being built locally. The river Severn probably had the most diverse fishing methods, each with its own type of boat. The seine-net – locally, a long net – was worked with a salmon punt upstream whilst downstream the stop-net boat worked stop-nets: a particular V-shaped net swung over the side of the boat facing the ebb.

Similar boats worked the river Wye. In Pembrokeshire, small, open compass net boats worked smaller versions of the stop-net. Coracles worked nets in various Welsh rivers whilst seine-net boats also worked other rivers such

▲ Small Cornish crab boats at Penberth. (Courtesy of John Robinson)

◄◄ Elliptical boats on the beach at Hastings.

➤ Typical motorised Suffolk beach boat at Aldeburgh in 1995. (Courtesy of Nicola Dixon)

as the river Dovey. The river Dee had its own Dee salmon boats, which worked under sail. The common denominator with all these seine-net boats was the aft shelf upon which the net was kept. Similarly, river Lune whammel-net boats fished the lower reaches of that river.

Ireland had a number of localised river craft, such as the mussel and salmon prams of the river Boyne, the snap-net cots of the river Slaney, the Checkpoint prongs, the Blackwater yawls and the Wexford river cots, the largest of which even worked offshore. The common denominator

⌃ Alun Lewis aboard his wooden compass-net boat, with net down, in 2015.

⌃ A Scottish salmon coble ashore. Note the upturned bow to cope with the surf when launching.

amongst these river craft was that they were all built locally, often by the fishermen themselves, and were built for their specific usage.

▼ A motorised Dee salmon boat at Chester in 2002.

➤ Raymond Rees, coracle fisherman of Carmarthen, showing how to carry a coracle on your back.

◄ Two small motorised Wick yoles in Keiss in 1998.

◄ Snap-net boats on the river Suir in 2007.

Industrial fishing is classed as commercial fishing undertaken on a large scale by large vessels. Pelagic trawlers fishing herring and mackerel out of Scottish ports are perhaps one of the best British examples. These large steel vessels, built outside the country, often work in pairs using mid-water trawls, which, as the name implies, is trawling in the water column anywhere except along the seabed.

Factory ships are also industrial fishing vessels and are usually stern trawlers. Freezer trawlers work the deep ocean and the catch is immediately frozen aboard. The world's largest freezing trawler by gross tonnage is the 144m-long *Annelies Ilena*, ex-*Atlantic Dawn*.

Built in 2000 for Irish owners, she was sold to Holland in 2007. She has been described as 'the ship from hell', so deadly is her ability to fish. She is able to process 350 tonnes of fish a day, can carry 3,000 tons of fuel and can store 7,000 tons of graded and frozen catch. She uses on-board forklift trucks to aid discharging. At the time of writing she was fishing 300 miles off the Irish coast.

Factory bottom liners fish use automatically baited hooks strung on long lines. Many thousands of hooks are set each day, the retrieval and setting of these being a continuous twenty-four-hour-a-day operation. These ships go to sea for up to six weeks at a time.

A purse seiner uses a traditional method of catching species such as herring and mackerel. A large net is set in a circle around a shoal of fish while on the surface. The net is then formed into a purse by closing the bottom of the net, and then pulling up the net until the fish are caught alongside the vessel. Most of these types of vessels then pump the fish aboard into refrigerated saltwater tanks. The fish are held in the tanks until unloaded, usually into a processing factory ashore. Purse seiners longer than 70m are called super seiners.

▲ The pelagic trawler *Daystar*, BF250, in 1999. Built in Norway in 1987, she was once pretty innovative. At over 160ft in length, she was full of modern technology necessary to find the shoals of herring. She had Refrigerated Salt Water (RSW) tanks capable of holding 300 tons of fish. However, by the early years of this century, she was almost obsolete as boats in excess of 230ft, able to carry 1,000 tons in their tanks, were the norm. (Courtesy of David Linkie)

GLOSSARY

Bow and stern	The ends of a boat.
Keel	The bottom bit, on top of which is fixed the rest of the boat.
Frames	The strengthening of a boat's hull.
Planking	The outside skin of a wooden boat.
Decking	The top bit that stops the rain going in.
Skin craft	Small craft made from a wooden frame with animal hide stretched over.
Clinker-built	Planks laid on top of, and riveted to, the preceding one.
Carvel-built	Planks laid side by side and caulked in between to keep the water out.
Square sail	A sail hung on a horizontal yard which is perpendicular (or square) to the mast.
Double-ended	Pointed at both ends, bow (front) and stern (back).
Transom-sterned	Having a flat or square stern at its aft (back) end.
Cutter rig	Having two or more headsails.
Sloop rig	Having only one headsail.

Ketch rig   Having two masts, the foremast higher than the mizzen mast.

Lugsail   An extension of the classical square sail where the yard is angled to give the sail a peak.

Gaff sail   A sail hung on a gaff which itself is wholly hung on the back of the mast.

Spritsail   The forerunner of the gaff where the leech of the sail (its aft edge) is supported by a spar called a sprit, fixed at its base to the mast near deck level.

Line-fishing   A system where a long string of hooks are fixed to the seabed and left over night. Two types exist: the sma' line and the great line, depending on depth of water, length of line, number of hooks etc.

Drift-net fishing   A long train of nets that is hung from the bow of a boat which is allowed to drift with the wind and tide.

Trawling   Where a net is pulled along in the water by a boat. Various methods are used.

Creel   A lobster or crab pot (usually in Scotland).

▼ Working boats in the days of sail evolved through many influences, both from home and other communities. These 'scaffies' off Wick show influence from across the North Sea.